# YOU AND I MIGHT BE SURPRISED

## RICKY CLEMONS

PUBLISHED BY FIDELI PUBLISHING, INC.

ISBN: 978-1-962402-46-0

Published by

Fideli Publishing, Inc.
119 W. Morgan St.
Martinsville, IN 46151
www.FideliPublishing.com

# Table of Contents

You and I Might Be Surprised ................................................... 1

How Did God Come into Existence? ...................................... 5

If People Go to Heaven After They Die ................................. 13

Jesus Sees No Color of the Skin ............................................ 20

Before I Knew God's Holy Word ........................................... 22

Deeper than the Deep Woods ............................................... 25

If it's in the Lord's Will ........................................................ 27

Reality ................................................................................. 29

It's Easy to Cover Up ........................................................... 31

Love One Another ................................................................ 33

Being a Christian ................................................................. 35

There is Nothing Good About .............................................. 37

You Don't Always Know ....................................................... 40

Repentance .......................................................................... 41

Grace is Undeserved Favor from God ................................... 43

We Must Choose Jesus Today ............................................... 45

We Just Don't Know When ................................................... 46

About the Bad Things .......................................................... 48

So Smart, Yet So Foolish................................................................ 50

When it Comes to the Lord............................................................ 52

All Wrapped Up in Jesus ............................................................... 54

The Devil Wants You to Believe.................................................... 55

Doesn't Come Anywhere Close...................................................... 58

Selfishness...................................................................................... 60

Without God's Love........................................................................ 63

# You and I Might Be Surprised

You and I might be surprised about who we see in heaven if we make it to heaven when Jesus comes back again.

Some people who might believe they will make it to heaven might not be there in heaven where Jesus will take you and me if we are saved in Him.

Some people who we might believe to be lost in their sins might be there in heaven with you and me because only Jesus truly knows all who will confess and repent of their sins before it's too late.

Only Jesus truly knows everyone's hearts and is not surprised about who He will take to heaven when He comes back again on the clouds of glory.

Only Jesus truly knows all who are saved in Him right now.

Only Jesus truly knows all who will become saved in Him before it's too late.

You and I might be surprised if we end up in heaven with Jesus when He comes back again because we don't truly know if we will make it to heaven.

We can only pray and hope that we will be in heaven with Jesus when He comes back again.

You and I might be surprised about who we might see in heaven and we might be surprised that we are there to not wake up in the second resurrection.

For death is only a short sleep to Jesus, who won't be surprised about waking us up in the first resurrection or in the second resurrection.

You and I might be surprised to wake up in the second resurrection unto eternal fire and brimstone that we will face if we are lost in our sins.

You and I just don't know if we are truly saved in Jesus, for we can only pray and hope that we will be in heaven because our works can't enter us into heaven, only Jesus can do that.

You and I can't believe that we are so holy and righteous and on our own way to heaven.

Only Jesus knows all of His true remnant children, so Jesus will not be surprised about who will go to heaven with Him when He comes back again on the clouds of glory.

Only we sinners saved through God's grace are prone to be surprised about anything, and especially about something going wrong when we believe to have it all together.

You and I might be surprised about who we will see in heaven, but we will be happy that they made it to heaven because of believing in Jesus Christ.

You and I will be happy that we made it to heaven but there will be some people who will be surprised to see you and me in heaven.

There will be many people who will be surprised to be raised up from the dead in the second resurrection.

Many so-called church folks will be surprised to be raised up in the second resurrection, where they will be lost in their sins to die again in the eternal death of hell's fire and brimstone.

Jesus will not be surprised about who will make it to heaven and who will go to hell.

Surprises are only for we imperfect human beings who were born with a sinful nature to sin against God who was not surprised about Lucifer and one third of the angels in heaven rebelling against Him.

No one can surprise God, who sees all and knows all things in heaven, in other worlds and in this world.

All existence would vanish away before anyone could surprise God, who was not surprised about Adam and Eve disobeying Him.

Hopefully you and I will be saved in Jesus and make it to heaven, where you and I might be surprised to see who we helped to make it to heaven with us.

Even though we might not know them or might never have seen them, we truly will be happy that they made it to heaven and be happy that we made it to heaven for believing in Jesus Christ.

You and I might be surprised about who we see in heaven because a wicked person who we know may confess and repent of their sins and turn to Jesus Christ during their last hour in this life before they die.

You and I might be surprised about some church brothers and sisters who aren't in heaven, but the Lord God is the supreme Judge who will show us why they didn't make it to heaven.

God will also show you and me why we made it to heaven.

Only the Lord Jesus Christ won't be surprised about who will make it to heaven and who won't make it to heaven.

One thing for sure, the righteous will make it to heaven and the wicked will go to hell and there will be no surprises about that because the bible tells us so.

You and I don't know all the people who are righteous to be saved in Jesus.

You and I don't know all who are wicked to be lost in their sins, but Jesus knows all who are righteous and all who are wicked and will not be surprised about who will enter into heaven and who will go to hell.

Jesus knows the heart of every person and they can't surprise Him, even though you and I might be surprised even about ourselves making it to heaven when we know that our righteousness is like filthy rags for only Jesus to make us perfect before God and His righteousness.

You and I, who claim to be Christians, might be surprised about waking up in the second resurrection among the wicked for holding on to even one unconfessed and unrepented sin that we can make excuses for and hold onto.

Not even one sin will enter into heaven before a holy and righteous God.

God won't be surprised to see anyone who He knows to love Him and keep His Commandments.

All who have lived in this world and are alive today might be surprised about their destiny to enter into heaven or enter into hell because God will judge everyone, dead or alive, and knows without any surprises about who will enter into heaven when Jesus comes back again on the clouds of glory.

You and I can only pray and hope that we make our calling sure in the Lord Jesus Christ while we are alive today, because chances will be slim for the righteous to enter into heaven where Jesus is not surprised about whose case He is pleading for before God.

You and I just don't know if our case has been closed already.

It's never good and wise for anyone to live their lives rejecting Jesus until they are on their dying bed and wanting to believe in Jesus because by then it might be too late for Jesus to not be surprised.

Only Jesus is not surprised about anyone being saved in Him in their last hour of life, but you and I might be surprised about seeing someone in heaven who we believe to be lost in their sins.

But if you and I don't make it to heaven, someone might be surprised to not see us in heaven, especially if we had convinced them to believe that we were Christians.

Only Jesus truly knows and isn't surprised that we missed out on heaven.

## I PETER 4:18v

# How Did God Come into Existence?

How did God come into existence?

Did God create Himself?

The bible says that God created the heavens and the earth.

If evolution brought everything into existence, then is it possible that evolution created itself from nothing?

Did God come from nothing?

No human being will ever know how God came into existence, because that is very impossible for all creations to ever know and fathom God's omnipresence and eternal existence.

We Christians depend on the bible that tells us about holy men and holy women who had an encounter with supernatural beings called angels who claimed to be sent from heaven by God.

The fullness of heaven was unseen by those holy men and holy women who believed in an unseen God who atheists see to be so useless to them because they believe that evolution created all existence.

Atheists would go insane before knowing how God came into existence.

We have eyes to see the things that exist around us.

We believe without a doubt that what we see is real and it exists to us.

We have experienced some things that we have seen, and you and I who believe in Jesus Christ have experienced God's love in Jesus who we have never seen.

We Christians believe that Jesus is extraordinary and above anyone and anything in this world.

We Christians believe that God is who He says He is and that it's God who is keeping us alive.

We exist by no coincidence, and we know we can trust this because all existence comes from God who is unseen by the naked eye.

Evolutionists are prone to claim that only the existence they can see is real, but there is so much more in existence that is eternal and that they cannot see because God created it.

Many people will put their theories above God, but their theories have no substance and are like the wind.

God has eternal substance, and the bible tells us that God created this world with substance.

Even atheists claim this world is real and they can see it with their eyes from day to day.

We Christians believe in Jesus Christ, and have seen lots of evidence that God is real.

He answers our prayers and He provides for all of our needs.

We Christians, especially, have experienced the power of Jesus Christ, who cleanses us from our sins so that we have no desire to commit those sins again.

God the Father, God the Son Jesus Christ and God the Holy Spirit is the beginning of all existence, seen and unseen.

Many atheists have returned to the dust of the earth and are nothing that God created all existence from.

We Christians don't need to know how God came into existence.

If we can't handle everything that exists to our naked eyes, then how can we handle the information about the origin of God?

Many angels fell from heaven because they took God for granted, acting as if God was beneath them and not worthy to be above their level of existing forever and ever.

How God came into existence is an eternal mystery to all of God's creations, and we will not be able to solve that mystery from eternity to eternity.

God is God who existed before all seen and unseen things that would vanish into thin air before God would tell anyone how He existed before all things.

How did God come into existence?

The existence of thousands of universes and trillions of galaxies is nothing in comparison to the existence of God.

How did God come into existence?

The angels are prone to receive eternal death and exist no more because of rebelling against God who will one day eliminate the fallen angels' existence.

How did God come into existence?

We human beings are prone to receive eternal death and exist no more because of rebelling against God, who will one day eliminate every wicked human being to prove that existence was created by God.

Evolution is only created in the minds of atheist men and women who believe that evolution created them to exist.

We Christians believe that a genius intelligence created us human beings to make choices, whether they're right or wrong.

We Christians believe that we exist because of God, but many people will create their own false gods that don't have anything to do with their existence and have no power to convict and convert a sinner to repent and turn away from living in sin.

How did God come into existence?

We don't need to know the answer to that question, but we can truly be thankful that God will exist forever and ever so that you and I can receive eternal life through His Son, Jesus Christ, who existed in the beginning with God.

Even before the fallen angels existed and rebelled against God, Jesus existed in God's eternal glory, power and majesty for all existence to worship Him who didn't force the angels to worship.

How did God come into existence?

All of existence can't come up with the slightest clue to answer this, and neither can you or I.

Our lives are like one second on the clock to an eternal God who created all existence from nothing.

Evolutionists make it seem like evolution is an eternal substance, but it only exists in their minds.

They cannot ever cause God to not exist to us Christians, or even to the animals that can sense God in their existence.

How did God come into existence?

History has existed with God in allowing the past generations to have a family tree today.

This is true especially for God-fearing Christians who pass down their faith in Jesus Christ to reach younger generations today.

How did God come into existence?

God existed in the technology back in the bible days when God gave Moses the technology to build an earthly sanctuary for him to dwell in among his people.

Evolution can't get rid of God, who existed before mortal evolutionists who knew nothing in their mother's womb when God knitted their bodies together.

When they were born, they did not know how to speak one word that makes good sense.

How did God come into existence?

Angels and mortal human beings can never figure this out because we are so low down beneath God in His eternal wisdom, knowledge and power that caused the fallen angels' temptations to be limited, especially upon all who believe in His Son, Jesus Christ.

If Lucifer had known how God came into existence, he would never have wanted to take God's place on His holy throne because he would truly know that only God is worthy to be God.

Lucifer would truly know that only God can handle being God on His holy throne.

Lucifer would have known that his existence would be so useless without God's existing eternal love for him.

How God came into existence is a question that only God can answer, and before God would answer that question all existence would pass away and be worthless to God's existence of eternal holiness, righteousness and perfection.

God's existence comes from God and the existence of eternity can't ever comprehend that.

You and I are well on our way to returning to dust as we age each day and get older in a fallen, sinful world where our lives only exist for a short time under the sun, especially in the presence of an eternal, existing God.

After we die, we can only exist again in Jesus Christ, the Son of God, who we must believe in to be saved to receive eternal life when Jesus comes back again.

For there will be no other kind of existence of life-eternal without Jesus, who existed with God and the Holy Spirit to create the heavens and earth.

How did God come into existence?

God is everlasting to everlasting, forever beyond you and me who don't know what living really is until we live in heaven with Jesus and exist forever and ever.

All the angels and unfallen worlds will know that God sealed our eternal existence in His Son, Jesus Christ, who existed before eternity, which would be very short without God's approval to exist forever and ever.

How did God come into existence?

God proves to all existence that He is love, even out of His strange act to one day destroy all the fallen angels and rebellious human beings in the lake of fire.

How did God come into existence?

God will take no desire to take pleasure in destroying the all wicked one day while forgiving you and me of our sins if we repent and turn to His Son, Jesus Christ, who gave us His life on the cross and rose from the grave to save us from our sins.

How did God come into existence?

God originated chance, and God gives us a chance to live for Him before it's too late, and that is the real, ultimate chance that only God can give to all human beings.

How did God come into existence?

Time does not exist for God, who came into existence when time had no meaning.

God created time here on earth to give us sinners like you and me no excuse to not give Him any of our time in prayer and service unto Him.

How did God come into existence?

Existence is nothing without God, who is not sitting down on His holy throne and doing nothing.

God is truly very aware and active in heaven and earth and in unfallen worlds that know God truly cares to keep His eternity sealed in obedient hearts unto Him.

How did God come into existence?

God has everyone's name in His book of life for believing in Jesus Christ, who the old books in the bible point to for His ultimate sacrifice for everybody's sins.

How did God come into existence?

No one can put themselves above God and live forever believing that existence originated from a big bang theory, which was an idea only formed in imaginative minds that are far from God's handworks of His creations.

How did God come into existence?

The naked eye can't see the unseen God in all of His glory that God had to keep away from Moses, who would have died if he'd seen God in all of His existence.

How did God come into existence?

The war in heaven could not eliminate God's existence, when mortal, wicked war mongers will strive to commit genocide against those they hate here on earth.

How did God come into existence?

Sin can never eliminate God's existence, and Jesus Christ truly proved that to all the holy angels, the unfallen worlds and to you and me who believe in Him, knowing that one day He will create a new heaven and a new world to exist forever and ever.

Jesus has truly proved that God will exist forever and ever beyond this fallen world that couldn't keep Jesus in the grave, and the grave will not exist for all the saints going with Jesus to heaven when He comes back again.

How did God come into existence?

God is the origin of existence, not evolution like foolish mortal people think.

They can't ever imagine the eternal truth of God that stretches out into the endless light years in countless unknown galaxies and universes beneath the highest heaven where God dwells on His eternal holy throne.

Astronomers are countless light years away from discovering the countless unknown in the outer space that is too small to contain God in it.

How did God come into existence?

God revealed His Son, Jesus Christ, in flesh and blood to sinners who would have dropped dead if Jesus had revealed His supreme totality to them.

How did God come into existence?

God's existence makes science look so dwarfed before the giant of God's eternal creativity that dissolves science into the capsule of this cureless world.

Jesus is our only cure in this sin-sick world where healing is permanent in Jesus, who can surely baffle the fields of science, technology and astronomy.

How did God come into existence?

We Christians won't question God about His eternal existence because His existence is love.

Regardless, many people will question God, especially if a loved one dies and doesn't exist anymore.

## EXODUS 33:20–23v

# If People Go to Heaven After They Die

If people go to heaven after they die, then the bible would be a lie for saying that Jesus Christ is coming back again to raise the righteous dead.

If people go to heaven after they die, then there would be no one in the grave for Jesus to raise from the dead.

The purpose of Jesus Christ coming back again is to raise the righteous dead and change the righteous living from mortal to immortal and take them to live with Him in heaven forever and ever.

If people go to heaven right after they die, then there would be no need for Jesus to come back again.

If people go to heaven after they die, then what is the use of putting their body down in the ground? That would be a waste of time.

If people go to heaven after they die, then why would they want to come down from heaven and reappear before you and me in this sinful world?

Why would they want to see you and me suffer in sickness when they can't be with us to comfort us?

If people go to heaven after they die, then there would be no need to bury anyone because there would be no body to bury.

If people go to heaven after they die, then there would be no one's body rotting in the grave because there would be real bodies in heaven, not people floating around in thin air.

If people go to heaven after they die, then what is the use of having funeral homes and funeral services if the dead wake back up again within the next day, week, month or year?

If people go to heaven after they die, then why would they want to reappear before us when they can't constantly be with us or do things with us?

That would be torture for them for God to take them to heaven right after they die, where they could see you and me going through hardships while they live on easy street in heaven looking down on us.

If people go to heaven after they die, then Jesus would have had no need to die on the cross for our sins that we can't take to heaven with us.

If people go to heaven after they die, then the bible would be so worthless to read and study about Jesus Christ coming back again on the clouds of glory to raise the righteous dead.

If people go to heaven after they die, then why would we waste our time grieving over our loved ones?

That would be so unfair to you and me for them to reappear before us who would be so very limited compared to their joy in heaven as we go through our ups and downs in this sinful world.

If people go to heaven after they die, then Jesus Christ would not be the Resurrection to raise the dead because there would be no dead to be raised.

If it was true that people go to heaven after they die, the devil would not waste his time killing people.

Why would the devil want people to go to heaven after they die, when that would mean he had a lost mission to destroy people?

If people go to heaven after they die, then the devil would not be able to take anyone to hell with him because everybody would be in heaven, whether they are good or evil.

The devil knows that he is going to hell and he is trying his best to take as many people with him as he can.

Jesus will raise the wicked dead and judge them to be cast into the lake of fire.

If people go to heaven after they die, then Jesus is a liar who won't come back again and raise the righteous dead and change the righteous living from mortal to immortal.

If people go to heaven right after they die, then why would anyone waste their time living in a very troubled, sinful world when they could be in heaven enjoying the eternal peace of God?

If it was really true that people go to heaven after they die, then everyone would want to die and leave this world so they could live in heaven.

No one would want to wait for Jesus to come back again because that would be a waste of time if we go to heaven right after we die.

The devil would just be wasting his time causing souls to be lost if people go straight to heaven after they die.

If people go to heaven after they die, then it would not make any good sense for the grave to exist and tombs would be so empty.

God says that we will return to dust after we die, but if we go to heaven right after we die then how can we return to dust?

We would have no need to be buried in the grave if we go to heaven after we die.

God is not that kind of God to allow you and me to go to heaven after we die.

God won't let us enter into heaven without Jesus taking us there when He comes back again.

Jesus' death on the cross would have been so worthless if we can go to heaven right after we die.

Heaven was wrapped all up in Jesus' death and resurrection that covers over everyone who ever lived in this world from the beginning of time.

There are people who are in heaven right now, and that's because of Jesus' profound reasons.

Those people who are in heaven didn't enter into heaven without Jesus being there with them.

They couldn't pass by Jesus and enter into heaven.

No one can leave Jesus out of their lives and go to heaven.

No one can go to heaven if Jesus is not there, and no one today will go to heaven before Jesus comes back again on the clouds of glory.

No one has ever entered into heaven without Jesus being there to accept them, just like He accepted Enoch, Moses, Elijah and those who Jesus resurrected from the grave when He rose from the grave and took them back to heaven with Him.

If people go to heaven after they die, then Jesus would have no purpose to come back again.

Why would Jesus tell us in His holy word that He is coming back again if there is no one to raise from the dead?

There would be no righteous dead that Jesus would raise and take to heaven with Him.

No one will go to heaven if Jesus doesn't come back again, and no one who is dead will be raised from the dead before Jesus comes back again.

The dead have no power to raise themselves after they die; they have to stay in the grave until Jesus comes back again.

None of our dead loved ones are looking down on us from heaven because they can't enter into heaven before Jesus comes back again to raise them from the dead if they are saved in Him.

When you and I die, we won't go to heaven after we die because we will stay right in the grave where we will know nothing until Jesus raises us from the dead when He comes back again on the clouds of glory.

After we die, we won't go to heaven and float around in the thin air without our bodies that Jesus will make new when He raises us from the dead to live forever in our new immortal bodies that will be real to touch and feel.

If people go to straight to heaven right after they die, then why would hell even exist.

It would be a waste of God's time to cast wicked people into hell if this was true.

Jesus will not take everybody to heaven when He comes back again, and surely no one can go to heaven right after they die because God won't accept them in before Jesus comes back again to raise the righteous dead who will truly know that Jesus raised them right on time.

If people go to heaven after they die, then why would time even exist?

It would be of no good use to anyone because time would never be too late for anyone to die and go straight to heaven with no need to wait on Jesus to come back again.

When Jesus comes back again that will be the real, true supernatural thing for only the righteous to enter into heaven and they will truly know that they didn't die and make it to heaven without Jesus raising them from the dead.

Many people believe that after they die they will go straight to heaven without Jesus coming back again to raise them from the dead.

Death and the grave truly know that they will keep us in the dust and we will know nothing and do nothing until Jesus Christ comes back again to raise us from the dead if we die being saved in Him.

If everybody goes to heaven right after they die, then why would our free will exist?

It would be so useless to God, who created us with a free will to choose to love and obey His Son, Jesus, who is our only way to enter into heaven when He comes back again.

If we go to heaven right after we die, then it will be so useless for Jesus Christ to be the head of the church, because we won't need Jesus to come back again if the righteous die and go straight to heaven.

The church would have no need to wait for Jesus Christ to come back again if we go straight to heaven after we die.

We would have no need to wait for Jesus Christ to come back again if we go to heaven right after we die.

We would have no need to sing any songs about Jesus coming back again.

Preachers would have no need to preach sermons about Jesus coming back again if we go to heaven right after we die.

The church would be so useless to go to and hear about Jesus coming back again to take us to heaven if we go to heaven right after we die.

This would make Jesus so obsolete to the church.

If the bible is not true when it talks about Jesus Christ coming back again to raise the righteous dead and change the righteous living from mortal to immortal and take us to heaven, then it's impossible for heaven to even exist if the bible is a lie.

The only truth is in the bible, because without the bible truth the church is lying for telling people that they will go to heaven right after they die.

The bible says that Jesus Christ is coming back again on the clouds of glory to raise the righteous dead and change the righteous living from mortal to immortal and take all to heaven who are saved in Him.

No one can get ahead of Jesus and go right to heaven after they die.

That is an insult to Jesus, who resurrected from the dead and went back to heaven to make a way for you and me to enter into heaven when He comes back again on the clouds of glory.

Fallen angels from heaven can appear to be our dead loved ones talking to us from heaven, and they can also appear to be our dead friends.

They have the power to deceive us that way if we don't read and study God's holy word and know the truth about only Jesus having the power to take us to heaven when He comes back again.

No one will go to heaven right after they die.

Without Jesus being in heaven, there would be no people in heaven beginning with Enoch who was the first one Jesus translated and took to heaven before Moses and Elijah, and before those who Jesus resurrected when he resurrected and went back to heaven.

No one else will go to heaven until Jesus comes back again on the clouds of glory like it says in Ecclesiastes 9:5, 6v and 1st Thessalonians 4:13-17v.

# Jesus Sees No Color of the Skin

Jesus sees no color of the skin because that doesn't concern Jesus; He will take every color of skin to heaven with Him when He comes back again.

The color of the skin doesn't matter to Jesus when it comes to giving eternal life when He comes back again.

The color of the skin is a big problem to controlling people who don't know what love is.

Jesus sees no color of the skin because Jesus loves everybody, regardless of their skin color.

The color of their skin has caused people to be disliked.

The color of their skin has caused people to be discriminated against.

The color of their skin has caused people to be treated unfairly.

The color of their skin has caused people to be disrespected.

Jesus sees no color of the skin, because skin color is no problem to Jesus at all from day to day.

The color of their skin has caused people to be hated.

The color of their skin has caused people to dislike themselves.

The color of their skin has caused people to kill themselves.

The color of their skin has caused people to lose their minds.

Jesus sees no color of the skin, no matter who you are.

The color of their skin has caused people to be killed.

The color of their skin has caused people to be depressed.

The color of their skin has caused people to be proud.

Jesus sees no color of the skin, which is a difficult thing to believe for many people, but not Jesus.

The color of their skin has caused people to feel superior.

The color of their skin has caused people to behave badly.

The color of their skin has caused people to do bad things.

The color of their skin has caused people to be unreasonable.

Jesus sees no color of the skin to give an abundance of life to those who believe in Him.

The color of their skin is causing hardships for people today.

The color of their skin is causing injustice to people today.

The color of their skin is causing strife for people today.

Jesus sees no color of the skin and will open the windows of heaven and pour out blessings upon anyone who returns faithful tithes and offerings unto Him.

The color of their skin is causing people to miss out on their true love today.

The color of their skin is causing people to be judgmental today.

The color of their skin is causing people to have mistrust today.

The color of their skin is causing people to be ignorant today.

Jesus sees no color of the skin to be His church bride.

Jesus sees no color of the skin to be His wheat in the church where the wheat and tares will grow together for only Jesus to separate.

No skin color can stop that from happening.

Jesus sees no color of the skin to prosper in this world, where the color of your skin is a threat to people who are insecure.

Jesus sees no color of the skin to be for you and not against you if you love Him and keep His Commandments that are for every color of the skin to keep day after day.

The color of their skin has caused people to tell lies to oppress equality even today, but Jesus sees no color of the skin and everyone is equal in His holy eyesight.

ACTS 8:26–39v, GALATANS 3:26–29v

# Before I Knew God's Holy Word

When I was a little boy, I lived in my grandfather and step-grandmother's house with my mother, little sister, one of my aunts and my girl cousins.

We all lived in a small two-story house in a peaceful neighborhood where everybody on the street block was friendly.

This was before I knew God's holy word.

My living conditions weren't so easy because at night I had to use a pot to discharge my waste in, and then dump it out in the backyard outhouse the following morning.

There was no indoor bathroom in the house.

I had to wash up in a bowl to clean myself up.

This was before I knew God's holy word.

My mother, little sister and I moved out of the house in the summertime and moved in with a middle-aged married couple who smoked cigarettes.

The husband also drank alcohol to the point of getting drunk.

This was before I knew God's holy word.

When my mother, little sister and I lived in the two-story house with the middle-aged couple, my mother worked a job to pay the couple for our room and board for the summer.

My mother, little sister and I moved out of the couple's house before the summer was over and moved into our own one-story apartment that was only a few blocks away from the middle-aged couple's house and my grandparents' house.

This was before I knew God's holy word.

When my mother, little sister and I lived in our apartment, I had to attend a different junior high school that was integrated with black and white students.

This was something new and different for me.

This was before I knew God's holy word.

I had no problem fitting into this new environment in the junior high school, and was there from sixth grade to eighth grade.

Even though I didn't know God's holy word, I know today that the Lord was with me, my mother and my little sister every step of the way in our lives.

I thank the Lord for blessing me and my sister to go to high school and graduate.

This was before I knew God's holy word.

When my mother, little sister and I lived in the middle-aged couple's house I had to sleep on a folding chair that could open up so I could lay down.

I had to sleep that way in the same room with the middle-aged married couple, with my folding chair bed placed at the bottom of the couple's bed.

It was hard for me to fall asleep because of their loud snoring.

I thank the Lord today that He kept a roof over my head, regardless of some sleepless nights.

All of this was before I knew God's holy word that was active in my life, my mother's life and my little sister's life even though we were ignorant to God's holy word.

I am so blessed today to know God's holy word that is all about my Lord and Savior Jesus Christ.

I was redeemed when I didn't know it.

I remember when my mother made me go to church during the time my mother, little sister and I lived in the married couple's house that was only a few blocks from the church that we went to on a Sunday.

I went to that Methodist church, but I didn't know God's holy word that the preacher talked about up in the pulpit.

I had heard God's holy word, but I just didn't know the true meaning of it until I joined the Seventh Day Adventist church.

The Lord had my name, my mother's name and my little sister's name on the roster of the Seventh Day Adventist church before we knew God's holy word.

The Lord foreknew that I would choose to worship Him on His holy Sabbath day of rest that everybody will not choose to rest on.

In my early childhood, I didn't know God's holy word because it wasn't taught to me in my home, but I'm so glad today that God winked His eye at my mother's ignorance, my ignorance and my little sister's ignorance of not knowing His holy word.

Everyone has a story to tell about the choices they make, whether they are good or bad, but the Lord is fair to everyone and will not interrupt anyone's free will choices.

This is only a little story of my past life that the Lord put here for me to love Him and keep His Commandments day by day.

Everyone who is still alive has a story to tell, and they have no excuse to leave God out of their story.

## ACTS 17:28–30v

# Deeper than the Deep Woods

When I was about eleven or twelve years old, I used to go out into the deep woods to look for bamboo stems to make a cherry shooter.

I had a friend who went with me out into the deep woods.

There were times when I saw some snakes in the deep woods.

One time I came across a copperhead snake that was about five feet away from me.

I thank the Lord today that the snake crawled away from me.

I was young and didn't know any better than to go out into the deep woods without wearing the proper clothes to protect my bare skin from the poisonous plants.

I was ignorant and didn't know what the poisonous plants looked like when I went into the deep woods.

I didn't know what poison ivy, poison oak and poison sumac looked like in the deep woods.

When I look back on those days, I truly see today that God's mercy and grace is deeper than the deep woods that God's mercy and grace brought me safely through.

I loved going into the deep woods looking for bamboo stems to make some cherry shooters.

I thank the Lord today that a bear never came across my pathway.

I thank the Lord today that I never got bitten by a poisonous snake or a poisonous spider.

I thank the Lord today that I never walked into poisonous plants in the deep woods that are not deeper than God's mercy and grace that was upon me who just didn't know.

God's mercy and grace were inspirational poetry in the deep woods where the Lord recited my life for me to live to see this day.

The deep woods set up traps for me that God's mercy and grace kept me from walking into in the deep woods.

When I look back on my young, ignorant life, I realize the deep woods were like a bubble that God burst to have no substance in my life today.

God's mercy and grace is deeper than the deep woods that I walked into with unknown knowledge of what bad things could happen to me.

I thank the Lord today that nothing bad happened to me in the deep woods where God's mercy and grace was upon me when I was young and didn't know any better than to go into the deep woods without wearing the right protective clothing.

My life and your life would be like the deep woods if we do our own will and not God's will.

Most people in this world would never want to live in the deep woods because they love to live among many people and socialize with many other people every day.

The deep woods are so closed off from society every day that most people would rather live in the wide-open spaces where they can feel comfortable and drive on the roads.

God's mercy and grace is deeper than the deep woods where poisonous plants, poisonous spiders, poisonous snakes and wild beasts will show no mercy and no grace upon you and me.

EXODUS 33:19v

# If it's in the Lord's Will

No mental illness can keep the Lord from restoring the mind if it's in the Lord's will.

No physical illness can keep the Lord from restoring the body if it's in the Lord's will.

No blindness can keep the Lord from restoring the eyesight if it's in the Lord's will.

No deafness can keep the Lord from restoring the hearing if it's in the Lord's will.

No muteness can keep the Lord from restoring the voice if it's in the Lord's will.

No disease can keep the Lord from restoring good health if it's in the Lord's will.

No brokenness can keep the Lord from restoring the heart if it's in the Lord's will.

No surgeon, no doctor, no psychiatrist, no psychologist, no nurse, no therapist and no chiropractor can override the Lord and restore everybody to health.

The Lord can use deformities, afflictions and brokenness to glorify His name.

The Lord can use something bad to make something good from it, but you and I can't do that if it's not the Lord's will.

No sickness can keep the Lord from restoring wellness if it's in His will.

No scientist can find a cure for any disease if it's not in the Lord's will.

It was in the Lord's will for many people to be restored after losing their minds, losing their eyesight, losing their hearing and losing their good physical health.

If it's not in the Lord's will to recover from any illness, then only the Lord truly knows what's best for anyone whose will can't rise above the Lord's will.

**JAMES 4:13–15v**

# Reality

Reality can truly hurt us because the bad things that happen to us are real and can be hard for us to deal with.

Reality is a hard thing for many people from day to day.

Reality can cause many people to take their own lives.

Many people have a hard time facing up to reality, and that causes many people to get addicted to drugs and alcohol and smoking cigarettes.

Reality is hard on many people and causes them to want to live in a dream world and neglect the real problems in their lives.

Many people would rather live in a dream world than face up to their realities in this world.

Reality is a good thing for anyone who loves to live in reality from day to day.

Living in reality is the best way to live.

Reality bows down and worships Jesus Christ, who was more real than anyone and anything in the world that He came to so He could redeem us back to God.

Lucifer lived in a dream world and believed that he could take God's place on His holy throne.

The truth of God's holy word is not only spiritual but it's also reality over the devil's lies that mean people believe to be real truth.

Many people live in the devil's dream world that's filled with nothing but lies to make them miss out on the realness of the abundance of life in Jesus Christ.

Reality is believing in Jesus Christ, who gave up His life on the cross to save us from our sins.

Death and the grave are only a dream, not reality when it comes to Jesus Christ, who will come back again and raise up all of His children who lived their lives in the reality of being persecuted for His holy name's sake.

Reality is truly living for Jesus on our good days and bad days.

Reality is truly loving Jesus and keeping His Commandments.

Reality is truly all about Jesus Christ taking away the devil's power and authority over the world when He rose from the grave with the victory over death and the grave.

Reality is from Jesus, who gave us the free will choice to believe in Him and live for Him or to choose to live in the devil's fantasies and lies.

God's holy word is reality for everyone in this world to live by in this world of many people who would rather live in the devil's make-believe than live in the reality of the truth of God's holy word.

Anyone in this world can face up to the hard realities in their lives if you and I have faith, hope and trust in Jesus Christ, who reality and fantasies will bow down to on judgment day.

All the hard realities, fantasies, make-believes and dreams will truly see on judgment day that Jesus is the judge over everybody because Jesus knows whose names are in His book of life.

## JOHN 20:1–30v

# It's Easy to Cover Up

It's easy to cover up the hardships that we've been through in our lives.

It's easy to not want to remember the hardships we've been through.

All the hardships we've been through in our lives can surely help encourage others to get through their hardships because as long as we live, everybody will go through some hardships.

It's easy to cover up the hardships that Jesus Christ, our Lord, truly brought you and me through, even though we might try to pretend that we never had it hard in our lives.

We can want to cover up what the Lord wants us to share with others to help them know that they are not alone in what they are going through in their lives today.

Many Christians will cover up their hardships and will believe that you and I are so wrong for giving our testimonies about the hardships that the Lord Jesus Christ brought us through.

It's easy to cover up our hardships and carry ourselves like our lives have always been like a beautiful red rose.

It's easy to cover up our hardships that Jesus uses to strengthen us.

It's easy to cover our hardships that Jesus uses to spiritually mature us so that we can be of the greatest maturity.

It's easy to cover up our hardships when we brought some of those hardships upon ourselves, sometimes out of ignorance, but the Lord was so merciful to bring us through those hardships.

It's easy to want to cover up our past hardships that should truly be about giving the glory and praise to the Lord who uses our hardships for good to encourage others.

The devil uses our hardships in a bad way, to discourage others and make people look down on you and me with scorn.

It's easy to want to cover up our hardships, but going through some hardships for Jesus' name sake will make it very hard for the devil to succeed in his false accusations against us.

It's easy to cover up our hardships that Jesus can surely use to bless other people's lives in ways that you and I can't ever imagine until we get to heaven and see those people thanking us for sharing our hardships with them.

Not only the good times but the bad times that we Christians especially go through can win souls to the Lord Jesus Christ who went through the worst hardships to save you and me from our sins that are so easy for us sinners to cover up and not confess and repent of.

## 2 TIMOTHY 4:5–8v

# Love One Another

Many people of the world love one another.

They treat one another right every day.

Many people of the world will treat us Christians right every day.

We Christians should truly know what it means to love one another in the church and also love the people of the world, but hate their sins.

Everyone who is of the world is not evil.

There are many good people of the world who wouldn't want to kill a fly on the wall.

Many of us Christians today were once of the world and we didn't have it in our hearts to do anything bad to anyone.

We didn't have it in our hearts to even plan to do something bad to someone we didn't like.

We Christians, especially, are supposed to love one another.

Many of us Christians weren't born and raised in a Christian home.

We were born and raised in a home being of the world and received love from our parents, grandparents, uncles, aunts, cousins and sisters and brothers who were worldly people.

Many Christians today will pretend like they have never been of the world and look down on worldly people as if none of them will repent and turn to the Lord Jesus Christ who loves everybody.

Love can be twisted up by many Christians every day.

Many Christians don't truly know what love is, especially when they're willing to give up on someone who they believe to be lost in sin.

We Christians must love everybody and believe every soul can be saved in Jesus Christ, who commands us to love our neighbors and not try to judge them by what choices they make.

We Christians must love one another and also love the people of the world.

We must put our trust in Jesus to separate the wheat from the tares.

We Christians must love one another and the people of the world because there are people of the world who will confess and repent of their sins and turn to Jesus before it's too late to repent.

## LEVITICUS 19:18v, MARK 12:30v, 1 PETER 4:8–11v

# Being a Christian

Being a Christian doesn't mean that we will never think wrong ever again, for we can think wrong on the spur of the moment.

Being a Christian doesn't mean that we will never say something wrong ever again, for we can say something wrong on the spur of the moment.

Being a Christian doesn't mean that we will never do something wrong ever again, for we can do something wrong on the spur of the moment.

Being a Christian doesn't mean that we will never make a mistake ever again, for we can make a mistake on the spur of the moment.

Being a Christian doesn't mean that we will never get sick ever again, for we can get sick on the spur of the moment.

Being a Christian doesn't mean that we will never have a sinful nature ever again, for we can have a sinful nature on the spur of the moment.

Being a Christian doesn't mean that we will never sin again, for we can sin against God on the spur of the moment.

Being a Christian means that we just don't want to live in darkness ever again.

Being a Christian means that we have turned away from living in sin that we don't want to live in ever again.

Being a Christian means that we don't want to hold onto even one sin ever again.

Being a Christian means that we want to be like Jesus Christ every day, and we do not want to be of the world ever again.

Being a Christian means that our lives have been changed and we want to deny ourselves and pick up our crosses to follow Jesus.

Being a Christian means that we believe in Jesus Christ and don't want to believe the devil's lies ever again.

Being a Christian means that we are saved in Jesus Christ and have no desire to turn our backs on Jesus Christ who gave up His life on the cross to save us from our sins, and Jesus will never do that ever again.

Being a Christian doesn't mean that we cannot fall by the wayside because a wheat can be uprooted in the church for being mistaken to be a tare.

Being a Christian doesn't always mean that we will always be a Christian.

Only Jesus truly knows and will not be surprised about you and me going to hell or going with Him back to heaven when He comes back again on the clouds of glory.

We need the Holy Spirit to help us to always be a Christian, and we can only be a Christian one day at a time to be like Jesus.

Being a Christian doesn't mean that we will never be tempted by the devil ever again and never give into his temptations ever again.

Being a Christian means that if we sin against the Lord, we will certainly confess and repent of that sin unto the Lord and have no desire to ever commit that sin ever again.

Being a Christian means that we don't want to commit those past sins again.

Jesus cleanses us of those past sins and casts them into the bottom of the sea.

Being a Christian means that we don't want to be like the devil because Jesus lives in us and we don't want to ever be like the devil ever again.

Being a Christian means that we will do the Lord's will and never want to do our own will ever again because doing our own will is not being a Christian.

Being a Christian doesn't mean that everything will be good in our lives all the time, but we will never want to put our trust in ourselves or anyone else except Jesus to work things out in our lives in a way that's for our good so that we never want to lean to our own ways of doing anything ever again.

**EPHESIANS 6:16–18v, 1 PETER 4:12–17v**

# There is Nothing Good About

There is nothing good about a man cheating on his wife and a woman cheating on her husband, no matter how weak the love is between spouses.

There is nothing good about a man abusing his wife and a woman abusing her husband, no matter how angry they might get.

There is nothing good about abusing your children, no matter how disobedient they might be.

There is nothing good about having sex outside of marriage, no matter how good your boyfriend or girlfriend treats you.

There is nothing good about divorcing your husband or wife for no good reason, no matter how boring you might think your marriage is.

There is nothing good about lying on someone, no matter how much you don't like him or her.

There is nothing good about overworking yourself, no matter how high your salary might be.

There is nothing good about being lazy, no matter how easy you have it.

There is nothing good about making plans without the Lord in them, no matter how good your plans are.

There is nothing good about eating whatever you want to eat, no matter how good the food tastes.

There is nothing good about staying up late at night, no matter if you're retired from work.

There is nothing good about turning your back on the Lord, no matter how much someone in the church doesn't like you.

There is nothing good about putting someone up on a pedestal, no matter how genius he or she might be, because no one is without sin except Jesus Christ.

There is nothing good about being proud, no matter how many accomplishments you have made in your life that belongs to the Lord.

There is nothing good about believing you are self-made, no matter how rich you are; the Lord allowed you to be rich and can take it away from you.

There is nothing good about believing you're worthy of the Lord's blessings, no matter how much you've tithed and give offerings.

The Lord does not need your money, it's like pocket change to Him who is forevermore richer than the richest people in this world.

There is nothing good about knowing God's holy word and not living it, no matter how high your office position is in the church.

There is nothing good about speaking eloquent words with no true heart of repentance unto the Lord, no matter how educated you are.

There is nothing good about not having complete faith in the Lord, no matter how much you pray to the Lord.

There is nothing good about judging anyone, no matter how long it's been since he or she has been to church.

There is nothing good about evangelizing to the world while being very critical of your brothers and sisters in the church, no matter how well you know the bible scriptures.

There is nothing good about assuming anything about anyone without knowing his or her true situation, no matter how much you believe you are right about someone who only the Lord truly knows.

You don't know everything about yourself and might be surprised by what you might do or might not do.

Only the Lord knows you and me completely, and the devil knows you and me better than we know ourselves so he can tempt us to sin unaware against the Lord.

There is nothing good about having a relationship with the Lord if you don't try to understand your spiritual brothers' and sisters' struggles, because we all live our lives together before the Lord every day.

There is nothing good about uprooting a wheat for a tare in the church, no matter how great your sermons are about the Lord, who truly knows all of His wheat.

You and I can mistake a wheat for a tare, but it's the Lord who does the pruning for spiritual growth in Him.

## EPHESIANS 4:17–32v AND 5:1–33v

# You Don't Always Know

You don't always know how people will be uplifted by the good words that you say to them.

You don't always know how people will be encouraged by the good things that you do for them.

You don't always know how people will be motivated by achievements you make before their eyes.

You don't always know how people will change their clothing styles because of the decent way you dress.

You don't always know how you can change people's lives for the better by the good way you treat them.

You don't always know who will follow in your footsteps doing good things by seeing you living right by example in their eyes.

You don't always know how you will bless people's lives by spreading the gospel of Jesus Christ to them not only in words from the bible scriptures but also most of all through your righteous body language.

You don't always know how people will be affected by you from day to day, but if you live for Jesus you will be a blessing to no telling how many people, causing them to confess and repent of their sins and give all of their minds, hearts and souls to Jesus.

**1 THESSALONIANS 5:12–15v**

# Repentance

Repentance is turning away from our sins every day because sins are never good for anyone to live in.

We have sins to repent of every day and we need to confess those sins to the Lord.

We don't see all of our sins from day to day, but the Holy Spirit will show us a sin to confess and repent of to the Lord if we are in-tune with the Holy Spirit.

We have seen sins and we have unseen sins that we were born into this world with.

For as long as we live, repentance is turning away from our sins every day when we confess them to the Lord.

We can never run out of sins to confess to the Lord, and we can never run out of sins to repent of unto the Lord.

This is something we must do every day, because we will always have a sin in our life to confess and repent of unto the Lord.

There are over a thousand ways to sin against the Lord, and we cannot count all of our sins that Jesus became on the cross in our place to save us from being lost in our sins.

Repentance is a lifetime thing to do, because even though we are saved in Jesus it doesn't mean that we will always be saved in Jesus.

Jesus wants to save us from our sins, but we must do our part to always repent unto the Lord, and we need to do that every day and ask the Lord to forgive us of our sins when we repent.

Repentance is not just a physical thing of making it right with the Lord, it's also an emotional, mental, psychological and spiritual thing of making it right with the Lord every day that we live because we will never run out of a need to repent.

Many people believe that repentance is only a one-time thing to do by the Lord, but there is always a sin that we need to repent of unto the Lord.

If sanctification is a lifetime process, then that truly means we need to always repent of some kind of sin in our lives.

We Christians especially know that we are not perfect, which means we have sins to confess and repent of unto the Lord Jesus Christ.

If we have the Holy Spirit, then the Holy Spirit will truly show us a sin in our lives that we need to repent of unto the Lord who loves to forgive us of our sins and cleanse us of our sins that we acknowledge to Him.

The sins that we are not aware of in our lives might be some of the many unseen sins the Lord has already covered with His precious blood that He shed on the cross for all of our seen and unseen sins.

Repentance is for life, because every day we have some kind of sin in our lives to confess and repent unto the Lord.

We will do this if we have the Holy Spirit, who will show us the truth about our condition for us to know that only Jesus was without sin when He lived here on earth among sinners like you and me.

If you and I have the Holy Spirit, then the Holy Spirit will always show us another sin we need to repent of unto the Lord Jesus Christ who loves to save sinners from being lost in sin.

## LUKE 17:3, 4v

# Grace is Undeserved Favor from God

Grace is undeserved favor from God.

God gives us a second chance that we don't deserve.

God gives us a sane mind that we don't deserve.

Grace is undeserved favor from God.

God gives us our needs that we don't deserve.

God gives us talents that we don't deserve.

God gives us air to breathe that we don't deserve.

Grace is undeserved favor from God.

God gives us the sunshine that we don't deserve.

God gives us food to eat that we don't deserve.

God gives us water to drink that we don't deserve.

Grace is undeserved favor from God.

God gives us life that we don't deserve.

God gives us the free will choices that we don't deserve.

God gives us His goodness that we don't deserve.

Grace is undeserved favor from God.

God gives us His love that we don't deserve.

God gave us His only begotten Son, Jesus Christ, that we don't deserve to save us from our sins.

God gives us His grace that we don't deserve.

God gives us His strength that we don't deserve.

God gives us spiritual gifts that we don't deserve.

God gives us prosperity that we don't deserve.

Grace is undeserved favor from God.

God gives us protection that we don't deserve.

God gives us the bible truth that we don't deserve.

God gave us a mind to know right from wrong that we don't deserve.

Grace is undeserved favor from God.

God gave us a heart of the freedom of our motives and intentions away from the devil trying to tempt us to sin that we don't deserve.

God's grace is what we will never deserve when Jesus Christ is truth and grace that God sent to this world where many people take God's grace for an excuse to live in their sins, even while calling themselves a Christian.

God gives us His forgiveness that we don't deserve.

God gives us good opportunities that we don't deserve.

God gives us His salvation that we don't deserve.

God gives us His healing that we don't deserve.

God the Father, the Son and the Holy Spirit created us in their likeness that we don't deserve when many people will act like an untamed animal.

Grace has always been in this world from the beginning of time.

God gave His grace to Adam and Eve after they sinned against God.

It was because of God's grace that Adam and Eve didn't drop dead after eating that unforbidden fruit.

## ROMANS 3:23, 24v AND 5:15v–6:1, 2v

# We Must Choose Jesus Today

We must choose Jesus today, because we aren't promised twenty-four hours to live without Jesus allowing it.

We must choose Jesus today, because that is all we have to live if Jesus allows death to overshadow us.

We must choose Jesus today, because we don't know if it's our last day to live.

We must choose Jesus today, because the dead don't know the living who have a free will to choose to believe in Jesus Christ today.

We must choose Jesus today, because we can't pick and choose who gets to live and who will be taken to the grave — only Jesus can do this for His reasons, which are always right.

We must choose Jesus Christ the Lord today, because God can close His probation on this world for Jesus will stand up and say that it is finished to let the righteous be still and the filthy be still.

We must choose Jesus today, because it might be our time to die and hopefully be saved in Jesus.

All the dead in their graves already lived their lives and experienced crying as babies, teen-aged life changes and adult maturity and immaturity.

Everybody in their right, mature mind can choose to believe in Jesus today, because the devil has no power over anyone's free will to not choose Jesus.

We must choose Jesus today, because today is only certain in Jesus and only exists with Jesus' abundance of life for all who believe in Him.

Today is not too late for the living to choose to repent and turn to Jesus.

**2 Peter 1:10, 12**v

# We Just Don't Know When

We just don't know when we will think wrong.

We just don't know when we will say something wrong.

We just don't know when we will do something wrong.

We just don't know when we will make a mistake.

We just don't know when something will go wrong.

We just don't know when we will feel some pain.

We just don't know when an accident will happen.

We just don't know when a dream will appear in our sleep.

We just don't know when we will get sick.

We just don't know when we will have to help someone.

We just don't know when someone will commit a crime.

We just don't know when we will die.

We just don't know when someone will make us laugh.

We just don't know when someone will make us angry.

We just don't know when we will sneeze.

We just don't know when we will cough.

We just don't know when something doesn't go our way.

We just don't know when someone will give us a smile.

We just don't know when we will get disappointed.

We just don't know when someone will stare at us.

We just don't know when someone will tell us a lie.

We just don't know when someone will offend us.

We just don't know when something bad will happen.

We just don't know when God will close His probation on this world.

We just don't know when Jesus Christ will come back again.

## MATTHEW 24:36v

# About the Bad Things

We don't like to talk about the bad things we did in our lives, because they make us look bad.

We have no problem with talking about the good things we did in our lives.

We all love to look good before one another, as if we never did anything bad in our lives.

If that was true, then Jesus would have had no need to represent our cases before God up in heaven.

We would have nothing bad against us and not have any sins to confess and repent of unto the Lord Jesus Christ.

No matter what bad things anyone says and does, no person loves to treasure those bad things unless they are downright wicked.

Only a fool would be happy about doing bad things to ruin people's lives.

No child of God would want to say or do anything bad.

Many bad people don't like to talk about what they've done because they don't want to look bad, especially before their loved ones.

None of us is innocent of never saying or doing anything bad, because all sin is bad and there is no little sin or big sin — all sin is the same in the presence of God.

You and I can assume things about someone without having the true facts and believe we did nothing bad by assuming.

We can believe that we know someone when we really don't and want to judge them, believing that being judgmental is not bad.

Who in their right mind would only talk about the bad things they've done?

Even foolish people will talk about some good things so they don't make themselves look bad.

The Lord is so good to us all, good and bad, but it's always wise to learn from our mistakes and speak good words and do good things in the name of the Lord who shed His blood on the cross to wash us clean of every bad thing that we've done and don't want to do today for living our lives unto Jesus.

## ISAIAH 53:6v

# So Smart, Yet So Foolish

A lot of people are so smart, yet so foolish.

A lot of people are so smart in making speeches, yet so foolish in doing bad things.

A lot of people are so smart in saying the right words, yet so foolish in not doing what they say.

A lot of people are so smart in making friends, yet so foolish in losing good friends.

A lot of people are so smart in making a lot of money, yet so foolish in overspending their money.

A lot of people are so smart in getting the truth out of people, yet so foolish in telling lies.

A lot of people are so smart in convincing people, yet so foolish in deceiving people.

A lot of people are so smart in making accomplishments, yet so foolish in living a wild life.

A lot of people are so smart in technology, yet so foolish in not using their common sense.

A lot of people are so smart in finishing what they started, yet so foolish in not taking good care of themselves.

A lot of people are so smart in going to church, yet so foolish in not having a relationship with Jesus Christ.

A lot of people are so smart in using their spiritual gifts in the church, yet so foolish in holding onto some unconfessed sins.

A lot of people are so smart in praying with excellent words, yet so foolish in quenching the voice of the Holy Spirit speaking the truth to them.

A lot of people are so smart in the bible scriptures, yet so foolish in misinterpreting the scriptures to suit their selfish lifestyles.

A lot of people do good works in Jesus' name, yet they're so foolish in not emptying out all of their hearts to Jesus, who wants our hearts because they cheer him the most every day.

**PROVERBS 9:10–12v AND 14:7–9V, MATTHEW 25:1-13v, 2 TIMOTHY 2:23–25v**

# When it Comes to the Lord

When it comes to the Lord, there is always more room for more and more sermons about the Lord Jesus Christ.

When it comes to the Lord, there is always more room for more and more bible school lessons about the Lord Jesus Christ.

When it comes to the Lord, there is always more room for more and more gospel songs about the Lord Jesus Christ.

When it comes to the Lord, there is always more room for more and more testimonies about the Lord Jesus Christ.

When it comes to the Lord, there is always more room for more and more poems about the Lord Jesus Christ.

When it comes to the Lord, there is always more room for more and more prayers unto the Lord Jesus Christ.

When it comes to the Lord, there is always more and more room for more worship unto the Lord Jesus Christ.

When it comes to the Lord, there is always more room for more and more dedication unto the Lord Jesus Christ.

When it comes to the Lord, there is always more room for more and more service unto the Lord Jesus Christ.

When it comes to the Lord, there is always more room for more and more reverence unto the Lord Jesus Christ.

When it comes to the Lord, there is always more room for more and more faith unto the Lord Jesus Christ.

When it comes to the Lord, there is always more room for more and more love for the Lord Jesus Christ.

When it comes to the Lord, there is always more room for more and more confession and repentance unto the Lord Jesus Christ.

When it comes to the Lord, there is always more room for more and more obedience unto the Lord Jesus Christ.

When it comes to the Lord, there is always more room for more and more trust in the Lord Jesus Christ.

When it comes to the Lord, there is always more room for more and more sanctification from the Lord Jesus Christ.

When it comes to the Lord, there is always more room for more and more spiritual healing from the Lord Jesus Christ.

When it comes to the Lord, there is always more room for more and more of the Holy Spirit teaching us the truth about the Lord Jesus Christ.

When it comes to the Lord, there is always more room for more and more denying ourselves and picking up our crosses to follow the Lord Jesus Christ every day.

When it comes to the Lord, there is always more room for more and more of the Holy Spirit to convict us and convert us mind, heart, soul and strength to the Lord Jesus Christ.

One day at a time is all that we can do for Jesus to save us from our sins each day.

When it comes to the Lord, there is always more room for more and more keeping our eyes on the Lord Jesus Christ, who is at the beginning and at the end of the road of our Christian journey.

Our trials are on every side of the road, trying to distract us from keeping our eyes on Jesus Christ who is determined to give us the victory on our Christian journey that Jesus owns every day to keep you and me on the right road for believing in Him.

## HEBREWS 3:1–6v, 12–14v, AND 4:14–15v

# All Wrapped Up in Jesus

Goodness, kindness, gentleness, joy, peace, temperance, patience, faith and love are all wrapped up in Jesus.

Equality and truth are all wrapped up in Jesus.

Strength, honor, greatness, knowledge and wisdom are all wrapped up in Jesus.

Grace, glory, praise, worship and obedience are all wrapped up in Jesus.

Victory, humility, forgiveness, and giving are all wrapped up in Jesus.

Salvation, holiness, righteousness and prophecy are all wrapped up in Jesus.

Life, the Commandments, mercy, and healing are all wrapped up in Jesus.

Reality, judgment, miracles, and respect are all wrapped up in Jesus.

Creation, angels, other worlds and all existence are all wrapped up in Jesus.

The church, the bible, the righteous and the past, present and future are all wrapped up in Jesus.

The devil, his fallen angels and his human agents are not wrapped up in Jesus, and Jesus will destroy them all in fire and brimstone one day.

God the Father and God the Holy Spirit are all wrapped up in the God Jesus Christ who will raise the righteous dead and change the righteous living from mortal to immortal when He comes back again on the clouds of glory one day.

HEBREWS 1:1–14vand 2:5–18v

# The Devil Wants You to Believe

The devil wants you to believe that it's all right to be unfaithful to your spouse.

The devil wants you to believe that it's all right to tell a lie.

The devil wants you to believe that it's all right to eat whatever you want to eat.

The devil wants you to believe that it's all right to have sex while not being married.

The devil wants you to believe that it's all right to marry someone in the same gender.

The devil wants you to believe that it's all right to be a homosexual.

The devil wants you to believe that it's all right to boast about yourself.

The devil wants you to believe that it's all right to be prejudiced.

The devil wants you to believe that it's all right to use someone.

The devil wants you to believe that it's all right to cheat someone.

The devil wants you to believe that it's all right to gossip.

The devil wants you to believe that it's all right to complain.

The devil wants you to believe that it's all right to abuse someone.

The devil wants you to believe that it's all right to hate anyone.

The devil wants you to believe that it's all right to kill anyone.

The devil wants you to believe that it's all right to show respect of persons.

The devil wants you to believe that it's all right to oppress the poor.

The devil wants you to believe that it's all right to rob anyone.

The devil wants you to believe that it's all right to be selfish.

The devil wants you to believe that it's all right to hurt anyone.

The devil wants you to believe that it's all right to make fun of anyone.

The devil wants you to believe that it's all right to be jealous of anyone.

The devil wants you to believe that it's all right to pretend.

The devil wants you to believe that it's all right to deceive anyone.

The devil wants you to believe that it's all right to try to control anyone.

The devil wants you to believe that it's all right to fuss and fight with anyone.

The devil wants you to believe that it's all right to treat anyone bad.

The devil wants you to believe that it's all right to overwork yourself.

The devil wants you to believe that it's all right to be lazy.

The devil wants you to believe that it's all right to live by eyesight.

The devil wants you to believe that it's all right to put your trust in this world.

The devil wants you to believe that it's all right to break God's Commandments.

The devil wants you to believe that it's all right to not believe in Jesus Christ.

The devil wants you to believe that it's all right to turn your back on Jesus.

The devil wants you to believe that it's all right to not study the bible.

The devil wants you to believe that it's all right to not live by the bible.

The devil wants you to believe that it's all right to do your own will.

The devil wants you to believe that it's all right to do evil.

The devil wants you to believe that it's all right to not forgive anyone.

The devil wants you to believe that it's all right to hold grudges.

The devil wants you to believe that it's all right to be unfair to anyone.

The devil wants you to believe that it's all right to believe that you are better than anyone else.

The devil wants you to believe that it's all right to put anyone down.

The devil wants you to believe that it's all right to live your life in sin.

The devil wants you to believe that it's all right to believe that this is the only life and there is no after life after you die hopefully saved in Jesus, who will give you and me the eternal life when He comes back again on the clouds of glory.

# JOHN 8:42–47v

# Doesn't Come Anywhere Close

The most beautiful skyscraper buildings don't come anywhere close to the beautiful new Jerusalem holy city that Jesus is building for all the saints to live in one day.

The most beautiful houses don't come anywhere close to the beautiful new Jerusalem holy city.

The most beautiful airplanes don't come anywhere close to the beautiful new Jerusalem holy city.

The most beautiful trains don't come anywhere close to the beautiful new Jerusalem holy city.

The most beautiful trucks don't come anywhere close to the beautiful new Jerusalem holy city.

The most beautiful cars don't come anywhere close to the beautiful new Jerusalem holy city.

The most beautiful furnishings don't come anywhere close to the beautiful new Jerusalem holy city.

The most beautiful museums don't come anywhere close to the beautiful new Jerusalem holy city.

The most beautiful parks don't come anywhere close to the beautiful new Jerusalem holy city.

The most beautiful jewels don't come anywhere close to the beautiful new Jerusalem holy city.

The most beautiful landscapes don't come anywhere close to the beautiful new Jerusalem holy city.

The most beautiful flowers don't come anywhere close to the beautiful new Jerusalem holy city.

The most beautiful women don't come anywhere close to the beautiful new Jerusalem holy city that Jesus Christ will bring down from heaven to the earth after all the saints live in heaven for a thousand years.

Jesus will raise up all the wicked dead and they will join the devil and his fallen angels on the attack against the new Jerusalem holy city.

Jesus will destroy them all in fire and brimstone for them to fail their attack against the beautiful new Jerusalem holy city that will be an eternal city for all the saints to live in and hopefully you and I will be there in that beautiful and great city.

The most beautiful hotels don't come anywhere close to the beautiful new Jerusalem holy city.

The most beautiful shopping malls don't come anywhere close to the beautiful new Jerusalem holy city.

The most beautiful restaurants don't come anywhere close to the beautiful new Jerusalem holy city.

The most beautiful cruise ships don't come anywhere close to the beautiful new Jerusalem holy city.

The most beautiful mountains don't come anywhere close to the beautiful new Jerusalem holy city.

The most beautiful islands don't come anywhere close to the beautiful new Jerusalem holy city that God will live in and the angels in heaven and creatures in other worlds will visit the beautiful new Jerusalem holy city forever and ever.

## REVELATION 21:9–27v

# Selfishness

Selfishness will bring on jealousy.

Selfishness will bring on envy.

Selfishness will bring on heartaches.

Selfishness will bring on greed.

Selfishness will bring on pride.

Selfishness will bring on trouble.

Selfishness will bring on sicknesses.

Selfishness will bring on hatred.

Selfishness will bring on injustice.

Selfishness will bring on oppression.

Selfishness will bring on murders.

Selfishness will bring on thefts.

Selfishness will bring on rapes.

Selfishness will bring on manipulations.

Selfishness will bring on inequality.

Selfishness will bring on prejudices.

Selfishness will bring on discrimination.

Selfishness will bring on division.

Selfishness will bring on crimes.

Selfishness will bring on lies.

Selfishness will bring on insecurities.

Selfishness will bring on misfortune.

Selfishness will bring on poverty.

Selfishness will bring on dishonesty.

Selfishness will bring on deceit.

Selfishness will bring on bondage.

Selfishness will bring on wars.

Selfishness will bring on death upon millions of people.

Selfishness will bring on fraud.

Selfishness will bring on rebellion against God.

Selfishness will bring on a heart of stone.

Selfishness will bring on favoritism.

Selfishness will bring on strife.

Selfishness will bring on scams.

Selfishness will bring on corrupt power.

Selfishness will bring on divided nation.

Selfishness will bring on divided church.

Selfishness will bring on being lost in sin.

Selfishness will bring on eternal death.

Selfishness will bring on nothing good.

Selfishness will bring on schemes.

Selfishness will bring on bad choices.

Selfishness will bring on stress.

Selfishness will bring on drawing attention to oneself.

Selfishness will bring on losing good friends.

Selfishness will bring on destroying families.

Selfishness will bring on losing respect for oneself.

Selfishness will bring on gossip.

Selfishness will bring on jesting.

Selfishness will bring on turning one's back on Jesus.

Selfishness will bring on criticizing others.

Selfishness will bring on not returning faithful tithes and offerings unto the Lord Jesus Christ.

Selfishness will bring on holding grudges.

Selfishness will bring on not loving Jesus and not keeping His Commandments.

Selfishness will bring on making false accusations against people.

Selfishness will bring on being unfaithful to your spouse.

Selfishness will bring on wanting to be right all the time.

Selfishness will bring on debt.

Selfishness will bring on all kinds of problems.

Selfishness will bring on cheating people.

Selfishness will bring on treating people bad.

Selfishness will bring on ruining people's lives.

Selfishness will bring on abandonment.

Selfishness will bring on abusiveness.

Selfishness will bring on disobedience.

Selfishness will bring on sorrow.

Selfishness will bring on denying Jesus Christ before anyone.

Selfishness will bring on wanting the glory and praise for oneself when only Jesus is worthy to get the glory and praise.

Selfishness will bring on nothing good, but Jesus is good all the time to save the worst kind of sinners if they repent and turn to Him before it's too late.

## ISAIAH 4:12–15v, GALATIANS 5:20v, PHILIPPIANS 2:3–11v

# Without God's Love

Who can be encouraged without God's love?

Whose dream can come true without God's love?

Who can be good without God's love?

Who can be in good health without God's love?

Who can prosper without God's love?

Who can live without God's love?

Who can be successful without God's love?

Who can achieve without God's love?

Who can do right without God's love?

Who can talk right without God's love?

Who can think right without God's love?

Who can dress right without God's love?

Who can walk right without God's love?

Who can make the right choices without God's love?

Who can get the victory without God's love?

Who can live right without God's love?

Who can pray without God's love?

Who has purpose in life without God's love?

Who can believe in Jesus Christ without God's love?

Who can go to heaven without God's love?

Who can help others without God's love?

Who can be cleansed of their sins without God's love?

Who can learn from their mistakes without God's love?

Who can wise up without God's love?

Who can be wise without God's love?

Who can be educated without God's love?

Who can be skillful without God's love?

Who can be strong without God's love?

Who can be obedient without God's love?

Who can be blessed without God's love?

Who can overcome their addictions without God's love?

Who can make it through their trials without God's love?

Who can love anyone without God's love?

Who can love oneself without God's love?

Who can love God without God's love?

Who can love their pets without God's love?

Who can understand anything without God's love?

Who can deny themselves, pick up their cross and follow Jesus Christ without God's love?

Who can work out their own soul's salvation without God's love?

## JOHN 3:16v, 1 JOHN 4:19v